Our little
Welcomed
Wish
come true!

To honor you, you have to honor others.
To honor love, you have to honor loss.
To honor success, you have to honor failure.
To honor unknowns, you have to honor knowns.
To honor dreams, you have to honor change.
To honor comfort, you have to honor discomfort.
To honor comfort, you have to honor sad.
To honor happy, you have to honor sad.

I honor you, in your journey of love, success,
unknowns, dreams, comfort,
and happiness. And I honor all you have
had to go through to get there.

-Leigha Huggins

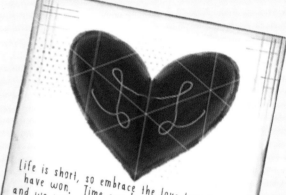

Life is short, so embrace the love lotteries you
have won. Time can be a fleeting moment,
and we must embrace those little moments that
one might miss. Take time to just lay there
with your little one, just a little longer. Hold
your loved one, just a little longer, it's ok to
put work aside and just sit there with your
little one, just a little longer. We'll always
have our love lotteries, but we won't always
have those moments. Enjoy those winnings
moments, whatever they may be.

-Melanie Darling

This book is given with love

_____

_____

Author: Leigha Huggins
Illustrator: Melanie Darling
Editors: Sam, Amy, Sheri, and Karen Austin

For all inquiries, please contact us at:
info@puppysmiles.org

To see more of our books, visit us at:
www.PuppyDogsAndIceCream.com

Love Lottery

Leigha Huggins

illustrated by Melanie Darling

Believing in love, believing in light,

desiring all that was wrong to be right.

Wishing upon the glittering sky,

with feelings of *trust* and a tear in my eye.

Pennies fell
from heaven above,
carried down by
a tiny white dove.

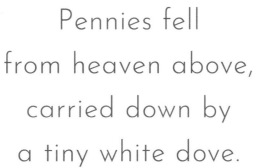

Stars then proceeded
to align.
Could they grant this

wish

of mine?

Just as the stars twinkled above,

the *clouds* joined in with teardrops of *love.*

Some things in *life* are just meant to be.

As your little *heart* called out to me

I couldn't
keep
my
joy
at
bay,
winning the
love
lottery
of you
that day.

Excitement
takes over,
pondering *life's* wins.

This is the story
of how
love begins.

Sunshine comes up,
and *happy* sets in,
beaming for you,
my *lottery* win.

Come with me, and we shall *dance*,

laughing as we *sing* and prance!

My child, however you came to be, I *trust* you were always meant for *me.*

Believing we
were never apart,
this *love*
runs wild
through my
heart.

Bringing a smile
from soul
to *face*,

sending
good vibes
all over
the place.

Our happiness forever leading the way,
of each and every

beautiful day!

Our

little

welcomed

wish come true,
did you choose us,
or did we choose you?

However our
stories
of *love*
are told,

they are
the tales
that
never
grow
old.

I will give you wisdom, comfort, love, and *truth*, to warm the innocence of your youth.

Sometimes *happy*
will come and go,
but it is *always* near,
I know.

So,

believe in happy

and honor sad.

Try to make good

even from bad.

Choose good thoughts when you think.

Life is only but a wink.

It's okay not knowing where all roads lead,
resilience and *love* is all that you need.

A silly *dance* to end our day, with thankful hearts as we play.

When you *wish* upon a star,

remember things

that aren't so far.

I wish you cheer. I wish you grace.

I *love* your darling, little face.

Thank you,
universe.

Thank you,
stars.

Thank you,
little one,
for being ours!

Sending *love* to *light* the *night,*

with *gratitude* for all that's right.

Follow us:
www.LoveHugsAndBooks.com

If "Love Lottery" has touched you heart,
we would love to hear from you!
Please consider leaving a review,
sharing a picture, or tagging us!

May your welcomes and love be abundant
throughout this journey of life.

@LoveLottery
#LoveLotteryBook

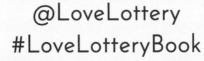

MEET THE AUTHOR

With love, purpose, and warmth, Leigha invites you into her world with her beautiful story. She is certain this message will resonate with you long after the pages of "Love Lottery" are tucked away. As Leigha guides her own Love Lotteries into the unknown, she always wants her love to be known, believing we are at our best when we feel loved and that words are the guiding force of life. She proudly presents you with this powerful little book to be enjoyed for a lifetime.

MEET THE ILLUSTRATOR

Welcome to the world of imagination, creativity, outlets, and wonder through the eyes of Melanie Darling! This talented soul displays her art all over her warm and quaint home, as well as the home of many across the world. "Love Lottery" was Melanie's first children's book, and Leigha can't thank her enough for her thoughtful, hard work.

Claim your FREE Gift!

Visit:

PDICBooks.com/Gift

Thank you for purchasing

Love Lottery

and welcome to the Puppy Dogs & Ice Cream family.

We're certain you're going to love the little gift

we've prepared for you at the website above.

Reed
Jamilet
Yanely
Austin
Sam
Heidi
Amelia
Amanda
Travis
Suki

Arianna
Alissa
Dennis

Love LOTTERY
Teryn
Lawrence
Alee
Bernadette

Harper
Braxton

Love LOTTERY

Evelyn

Joe

Love LOTTERY
Hudson
Lily
Isla

Nicky
Love LOTTERY 2020
Gracie

Julie
Sienna
Alec

Clemi
Brian
Ga

Love LOTTERY
Blazer
Huxton
Laila

Kellie
Love Lottery

Kora
Brooks
Lila
Karen
Maxwell
Evy
Ally
Rachel

Delka
Love LOTTERY
Calvin

Bella
Peighton
Joaquin
Michael
Sydney
Cai

Conner
Lisa
Lexi
Lilah
Love LOTTERY
Brody
Wil

Flynn
Avery
Love Lottery
Teaspoon
Amy
Everett

Kiran
Heather
Alex
Love LOTTERY
Adam

Sean
Brent
Rowan
Andrew
Lex
Carmen
Love LOTTERY

Aria
Doc
Love Lottery
Shay
Ansel
Austra
Josh
Troy

Love LOTTERY

Jillian
Scarlett
Landon
Justin
Luis
Cora
Nate
Clara
Lyla
M

Love LOTTERY
Dapnhe
Teagan
Love Lottery

Merida
Love LOTTERY
Chris
Miles

Jade
Joey
Ansel
Georgia
Beth
Kristi
Willie

Jax
Julian
Shiloh
Sage
Carrie
Raelee